THE GLEAMING OF THE BLADE

Editors' Selection from the 2021 Frost Place Chapbook Competition

THE GLEAMING OF THE BLADE

poems

CHRISTIAN J. COLLIER

BULL★CITY
PRESS

Durham, NC

The Gleaming of the Blade
Editors' Selection from the 2021 Frost Place Chapbook Competition
Copyright ©2021 by Christian J. Collier

Library of Congress Cataloging-in-Publication Data

Names: Collier, Christian J., 1983- author.
Title: The gleaming of the blade : poems / Christian J. Collier.
Description: Durham, NC : Bull City Press, [2021]
Identifiers: LCCN 2021045211 | ISBN 9781949344301 (paperback)
Subjects: LCGFT: Poetry.
Classification: LCC PS3603.O447 G57 2021 | DDC 811/.6--dc23/eng/20211006
LC record available at https://lccn.loc.gov/2021045211

Published in the United States of America
Book design by Spock and Associates

Cover artwork: "Strange Fruit" by Nathaniel Austin (*ArtbyNFA.com*)
Author photograph: Ian Riley Photography

Published by BULL CITY PRESS
1217 Odyssey Drive
Durham, NC 27713
www.BullCityPress.com

CONTENTS

THE GLEAMING OF THE BLADE

HOW IT FEELS TO BE BLACK

Sometimes, it feels like we are loved by no God,
like there is no gospel living in the gusts of wind that comb our cheeks.

The Word doesn't unmaim us, or leave us exempt from the wolves who always arrive blood-hungry.
Each day, I want to wake to find no name of someone Black & butchered in my throat, but

the morning never yields to my request,
so, more days than it should,

it feels like a bounty latched to the bleached rails of our spines,
like we are destined to keep dying unarmed & at fault,

like even angels have abandoned the fat lagoon of our skies
& Heaven,   Heaven will not have us.

WHEN MY DAYS FILL WITH GHOSTS

There are corpses on the streets of New York. Ambulance song in the air
every few minutes. I am groundless when a friend tells me
██████ is dead. I keep thinking of his three sons, how his low voice now must live in memory.

*

██████ is dead. I watch the last few seconds of his life in landscape mode on my cellphone.
I know, then, I have had enough. I can never willingly see the end for anyone else Black.
I am too full on death to want to witness any more.

*

██████ is dead because of the police.
I haven't breathed deeply since February.
I haven't let a night pass without crossing my body in the dark & begging God to intervene.

*

Holy, the spirits.
Holy, the Grey Goose, the Elijah Craig Small Batch.
Holy, the Patrón that awakens the burn in my throat, my chest, my liver.
Holy, the touch that brings, for a moment, the bite of something more than dread.

*

The fever comes one summer night.

Unsure if this is only regular sickness or the sickness that killed ██████.

I start imagining my life without me. After I sweat through the cotton bedsheets,

I tell the swaying shadows I am afraid to die—   to live air-hungry,   then not at all.

*

The next morning,
I take the interstate into Georgia & don't think about where to stop or turn around.
I want to commit everything the sun holds to my blood
in case the dark comes in the next two weeks.

*

The day after the election,
someone white throws our morning paper onto the roof of my family's home.
Someone white, again, wants us not to have what is ours
because of the spirits they cradle inside them.
My family has been Black & Southern long enough to expect this.
The spirits parading inside us won't let us forget or be surprised.

*

The spirits parading inside us won't let us forget or be surprised when the president won't concede.
Where we live,
when white people cannot accept the world,
often, it means the world will burn.

*

After my ▮▮▮▮ dies,
my ▮▮▮▮ tells me my ▮▮▮▮ can't stop sobbing.
I don't hear him, but knowing he is mourning unknits me.
I don't remember the last time he's been this exposed, this human.

*

Hours after I bend my knee in the late fall & ask my love to marry me, my ▮▮▮▮ dies.
I am afraid to cry, to open myself, to give any emotion to this barbed, new world.
I am afraid of the release, of feeling empty if it all oceans out.

*

The year ends
with fireworks in the distance & Johnnie Walker Black Label
in a Styrofoam cup. The year ends.
My dead are still gone. The year ends.
I've yet to stop feeling the brown earth dying beneath my feet.

BENEDICTION FOR THE BLACK & YOUNG

Children, we occupy a world not made
    to carry any of us.   Find the slivers of calm
        in the ash-filled air.   Breathe.
Do you feel the atoms coming apart around the garlic-white brims of our halos?

                  We are living through a time that took touch   from us,
        wading through the stubble of the burning night, finessing our feet forward
                                        as best we can.

                                      Let us pray
          there is a just God at the end of all of this.
Let us pray He sees the columns of our dead on the sour buds of the street, then stirs & says *enough*.

  Let us pray the liquor that drags us from the bed of one day & into the next does not run out,
  pray the Hennessy & Crown stays put,   pray we can also do the same sane & intact.

  Let us lay down our blues & not cross the threshold of another morning howling
  for those we could not see buried.

Let us pray for the favor of the big sky,   for burgundy wings
      no longer tucked beneath our shoulders & a sheath below
          the twitch of the stars.

Let us bow our heads & dream
a life that loves us better.   May it be gold-hued.

          May our minds sculpt a love supreme that also holds

our newborn ghosts.   Let us whisper,
because history says whenever someone Black wonders aloud about
the future, it instantly becomes a bruised sea of days they will never know. Children,

if we are only meant to forfeit
all that has ever known our names,
let us fraternize with
the condors who will come to escort us away.
Let the stomp of our forelimbs be
the last bit of grace
we grant this earth.

Then, let us rest well.
Let us be.

THE QUIET STORM

The officer's gun still awakens me
      fifteen years after the night
his index finger became a cedar ring around the trigger.

      Anytime I close my eyes, the muzzle's round cavity is trained on me.
Anytime rest takes hold, my mind expects the bullet—the sharp burst of light & noise.

      Because it does not come,
I live
      within a wound no one else can see. Trauma
builds its monsters
      from the bones of experience. Blood
records & remembers everything it survives.

      What did not kill me,
I now belong to. What has allowed more time to pass through me,
      I am possessed by. What owns me:
an ebony Glock 22 & a man's featureless face shouting
      behind a brass badge.

My almost-murderers breathe
      inside me.

I hear grit rustling in their throats at all times.
      Some songs never sleep.

WHEN THE MOON COULDN'T BE FOUND

John Coltrane seized my ear with the sound of his horn
as my girlfriend's father followed me out of Graysville after
he threatened to blow my head apart if he caught my brown hand upon her again.

The fog's silhouette shook its head
while I barreled through its shame.
It was witnessing, again, a Black man stalked

on a dark strand of Southern road. At 3:37 in the morning,
I was a blue locomotive rage blew from one white town to another
under a moonless sky. Coltrane was playing

& I wanted nothing but to be the rush of notes
surging from the speakers, painting the shaded inside of my Dodge Intrepid.
I wanted to be that free, that anointed by the sweet mouth of a dead god.

THE STANDARD

"My name is my name!"
    —Marlo Stanfield

The white woman at work's mouth is thin-lipped, never fully closed. My name doesn't fit inside it.
    Her roving tongue tears the letters apart,
        reconfigures them into the notes of a song I've not known.

Her mouth says the funniest things
    behind my back   to our colleagues.
She colors me disrespectful

    because I refuse to answer to a name that has never belonged to me.
She gives me the well of her ugly to stare into.
    I give her no satisfaction nor surrender.

    The mute reply. I keep the chapel of my jaw sacred.
    What's in my silence is
    a creek filled with my family's blood.

What's in a name except
all my mother & father hoped for when they knit themselves together?
    What's in a name except

every god of my past   still washing the dust from my soles?
    Every vanished god I give thanks to by going into the tomorrows that will have me,
    cradled in the closets that sit between the gums & the teeth.

CANDYMAN BLUES

Think of the commitment it takes
to call any one name five consecutive times.

Think of the desire at the heart of making it a mantra.
What they call me is a sacred word built on blues & blood

like any Black man born & buried in the South.
They say *Candyman* enough times & I am obliged to appear,

because they made a god out of me.
How could I not come when summoned?   When prayed to?

How could I not grant them their wish
to see my face? Mine, the last they'll see.   Mine, their guide away from this life.

Many call me
                                    monster.

Who made me into one?
          What name should we ascribe to those whose brutality transformed me?

If I am what they say I am,   it is because I did not know my place back then,
          because I made love to a white woman, molded a daughter in the kiln of her womb.

Before I became a monster on their tongues, I was the monster drinking in their sun.
          Now, my place is in the dark.

The shadows & I keep company
until the anxious chant of a curious mouth calls me out.   Now,

I live in the whispers of my congregation,
in the quiet notes of their barely-breathed hymns.

CANDACE

"One doesn't stop seeing. One doesn't stop framing. It doesn't turn off and turn on. It's on all the time."
        —Annie Leibovitz

Distance & time are
the midwives of acceptance.
We made our peace quietly with
who we were all those years ago.
We were vulnerable, thin ice just learning
the true weight of our care for one another,
when we both understood I had the heart to love you,
just not the skin. Life is what hands us our ghosts
& like anyone who has not yet died, I am
haunted country.
A field of blood polluted
by what I have lived beyond
flows behind my breast.

You never knew
I used to clasp my hands & pray for God to grant me a different world to wake to
where I could have you without secret or consequence.
This same sad earth was the only one
that desired anything to do with me.

I have never had far to reach to recall the word *nigger* lurching from your father   or your eyes
in the wave of the dark
the night you asked me to leave your seventeenth birthday party so your parents wouldn't know

14

I had come to celebrate.   Those memories
are carved atop the faded blue crowns of my veins.
The wounds I've grown to bear.   The wounds that won't leave.

INDOCTRINATION

for Rebecca

Do you remember?
                                We defied every angry eye fixed upon us

inside that diner, the scent of sizzling pork in the air.   Those stares said
        the region's ghosts were still alive—

                my flesh belonged too much to the sun to be with you.
We sinned & stood guilty,

        betraying our complexions
                        before the quiet ire of the jury. Our presence

was treason. You were from the North & didn't know the language down here, the field of thorns
        you had waded into,   how being a white girl with the wrong-skinned man

                was the equivalent of dancing in front of the dark O of a cannon's mouth,
listening to a flame chew away at the coil of a fuse.

THE APPETITE

I told Miranda it was the strangest thing—
    when her friend messaged me to say *I'm gonna kick your ass you fucking n,*

it seemed, for some reason,
    he couldn't bring himself to type out the other letters of the word nigger.

He left just the *n* stranded
    like a small piece of a glacier shaved away from the body.

I couldn't imagine how it must feel to be him—wanting to be seen as ugly, slightly
    monstrous, but lacking the bite, lacking the true taste for blood.

CHATTANOOGA BLUES

"Home is not where you live but where they understand you."
  —Christian Morgenstern

I have seen too much of this place & its people to feel truly comfortable here.
I have known the face of the darkness that lives within the city limits, stared into its eyes

& perhaps, that is why I have such a difficult time calling this home—
my tongue is barely even able to hold that word steady, small in
the arena of my mouth

the large rebel flag that stands, to this day,
like a sentinel outside the tiny brown house
across the street from the elementary school
where I play basketball— or the cotton
     a white stranger quietly dropped in my father's lawn
      one night while my family slept
        to remind us
        of our place,
  not to dream too brightly— or the manager of the small café downtown
          telling my Caucasian friends
       if they did not do something quick & decisive,
        Black people would claim & corrupt
         the very soul of the country—

all of this, all of these deep blemishes still remind me of the gospel of
my mother. She once told me never to fall in love
with something or someone incapable of loving me back.

I cannot recall how many years my body has remained
outside the full caress of this place.
It grew weary, ages ago,

for the day when this city,   this almost home,   could show me
its wide heart had finally tired of laboring
to mute the percussive music of mine.

A BLUES FOR THE WALNUT STREET BRIDGE

"There are wounds that never show on the body that are deeper and more hurtful than anything that bleeds."
  —Laurell K. Hamilton

For so many of us here in Chattanooga, we are guilty of forgetting
        Ed Johnson's & Alfred Blount's names still rest

on the back of the bridge's Quaker-blue tongue.
        After all this time,

the dense weight of their hanging bodies still haunts its broad girders.
        We never stop to wonder

if it rues that it was made
        to bring about their brutal ends.

It was forced to feel
        the life sifting away from their flesh & muscle.

I want to know if it envies
        how we, who casually walk across it, claim ignorance as a shield,

how we choose not to be burdened by the history that has stained it,
        how we work ourselves to the highest states of negligence

to avoid hearing the blues it, alone, has had to bear.

SIGHT UNSEEN

after viewing Hank Willis Thomas's "From Cain't See in the Morning Till Cain't See at Night"

Look.
    They insert the ▮▮▮▮ body, then count the minutes
before they can laud the rusted light pouring through its exit wounds.

      When they insert the ▮▮▮▮ body,
they must also make laws to govern the tone of its breath, limit its reach,
    then they beg it not to be so ▮▮▮▮
       it protests
          when they border up the air.

They insert the body & ask that it just be the ▮▮▮▮ that is all smiles,
full lips & teeth totally exposed.
The ▮▮▮▮ that pulls laughter from their guts instead of ire.
The ▮▮▮▮ that chooses not to let them see how they've exotified & commodified its labor
in the sun-kissed flex of its muscles.

      Ask that it be all spectacle,
bigger than life & mute about the realities it faces
& if it can't be,   can't it just be so ▮▮▮▮ it is invisible again?
So dark the night eats it away, buffing it from their sight?   Can't it
be the ▮▮▮▮ that loves them enough to keep the language of its lesions distant from their ears?

Can't it just repay them for the opportunity to play &
      produce, with enjoyment?

Can't it only kneel in victory, on occasion,
        praise the God they say they follow, on occasion?
Can't it be that broad-backed █████ buck just happy to have the green field all to itself?
        Can't it just let them step back & love it from afar, with conditions,
before it breaks down before their eyes, before the season sets on it?

If it can't bear to be that type of beautiful,
        to grant them absolution, all the splendor they can drink from its sweat & sacrifice,
can't it just shut up & dribble, or shut up & run, or shut up altogether,
        because they don't need the music of its mouth mangling their cheering?
Can't it just shut up & lie down against the earth its flesh has known so well,
        play dead so long & believably
it forgets

                how to get back up?

DWB

When I was a teenager
I sat in a conference room surrounded by other brown boys.
Our eyes were fastened to the glass face of a television screen
as the tape of Rodney King's beating played.

The only sound there with us was the dry wheeze of the air conditioner
as we inhaled each strike of the black baton against his flesh.

Our fathers exposed us to the sight of a brown man being torn down by the hands of the police
to teach us a lesson about survival.
                    The unwritten rules for driving while Black   could be
what preserved our living breaths.

They wanted us to know how dire the consequences could be
if we found ourselves behind the wheel in an exchange with the law.

Even one wrong pant could   be the last move we would ever have the chance to make.

Caution must be a second language kept   at all times   close
like the fine hairs hunkered on the cape of the neck.

WHEN SHE ASKS WHAT I'M AFRAID OF

I tell her:
someday, when the stout emotion of an argument has caught us,

the word nigger will be a bullet fired from her mouth, cast
for no other reason than to leave

me gutted before her.
She asks if I truly believe she would be capable of such a thing, could ever wish

to hurt me so much
she would say that barbed grave word.

I pause for a moment, then peer into the dark blue brooks of her eyes & lie
when I tell her no.

TOUCH

The dialogue dies
    when we exchange pictures.

After the brown psalm of my body soars across the city & appears on the face of her cellphone
    the dozens of spirited bones in her hands fall

    permanently mute.
        That temporary Eden we had been speaking so excitedly about finding together,

the sand-studded shore
    neither of us would ever reach.

    Like so many other nights,
    the tepid fondle of the moonlight is the only white thing that will or wants to touch my skin.

INDUCTION

A white couple at a bar smelled the bull in me
before even I knew it was there. Eating grain & grass, listening to a parade of birdsong.
They fed me four rum & Cokes, then clutched the metal ring in his nose, led us to a house
eight miles away from a bridge where two Black men were hanged. Here, in this Southern city,
everything black is both loved & feared: The night.   The soil.   Dick.

The bedroom is where I learned
pleasure requires surrender, a giving in,
an offering of blood.
While her husband watched from the corner,
she bit a small hole in the crown of my shoulder.

The animal—horn-headed, ruby-eyed—galloped out to be praised & in turn, praise.
Would you believe me if I said it was holy? While sinew & bedspring were pushed to near fracture,
she chanted the word *God* so many times, He hovered into the room, a pale flame with no shadow.
Would you believe if I said, when we finished, the light vanished &
forty cut roses were bent in prayer on the carpet?

FOLLOWING THE SHOOTING

I watched my four-year-old nephew sleep beside my mother, amazed by the beauty, the innocence

held within his resting face.
I could not stop thinking about the world's brutal language—

all the brown bodies wrongfully taken & buried in the fascia of the earth.
Thick with wonder, I entered the room, bent & kissed him, held

my lips against the floor of his forehead
before pulling away & whispering

to the Divine
I would gladly barter my remaining breath

if He would promise
to watch over & shield him.

I asked that He promise
to hold him in His grace like a high note & only claim him after a long life well-lived.

When I heard nothing back, no holy voice answering
in the low-lit room,

I pleaded, with tears burning the round jewels of my eyes,
for God to grant my nephew mercy.

DEAR GOD

When I brought my hands together,

bowed my head,   closed my eyes   & began to pray,
I told God I hoped everyone in the midst of the shooting would be alright & protected,
even though in the hull of my gut,   I knew they wouldn't be.

I asked that grace be given
                to the victims,
                to the officers on the scene   & all their families & friends.

I asked that the perpetrators of this, the harbingers of this disaster, would come to justice quickly.

The last thing to exit my lips & find His ear surprised me though,   jolted my entire body.
I felt slightly ashamed when I asked

        that the shooters not resemble me,
        that their skin not be too dark or
        that their names not sound too strange to the American tongue.

I pleaded to remain outside of this,   unmarred & blameless,
not in the eyes of the Almighty,   but in the eyes of those around me who claim to follow His path.

ELEGY FOR JULIUS GAW

Even though I've seen the scene   well over thirty times   & know   how it ends,

I still have hope in my cells

this will be the time   some miracle will reach through the screen & save him,

though he faced death

on the ashen clavicle of that Manhattan building

before the lone audience of the moon,

he will somehow will his exhausted body into slipping that fatal Sunday punch

to escape free,   unsmudged & alive.

Perhaps it is just

the world refusing to let me be,   to stay out of my head for the runtime of the film, but

I also cannot help thinking about

the other Black boys not hired by a casting director to be rendered headless on film,

those now forever anchored to being young,

whose families were elected by the god of circumstance

to carry the murders of their sons   or fathers   or brothers

    the remainder of their days.

How many times have I seen the soul of someone Black exit

the pores of their tiny mosques of muscle & flesh, vacating this life?

    Each of their final moments was a horror film I did not pay to see & cannot let go of.

      In some way,

isn't this   the nature of being Black   in America?   Always residing so close to terror,

we are wounded,   but never surprised,

    when it pitches one of us into the limbo of its maw?

           Me, I want the alternate ending,

        not just for Julius, but

for all the other young Black men buried in my brain, each one

    tucked into the pink soil of my mind.

I want the alternate ending,

    a burst of lightning   blossoms & brings them life again &

they gaze into the black eyes of their fates   & say   *Take your best shot, motherfucker*

before punching their hands bloody
staving off the afterlife's hungry invitation.

I want the alternate ending where they find their ways back into the graces of their most-loved.

In the distance,

night bleeds away   & a brand new beginning sets upon them.

As the credits cascade down the screen,

the language left on their breath is the antithesis of horror,

of anything close to horror.

NOTES

"Candyman Blues" is a persona poem written from the perspective of Clive Barker's character Daniel Robitaille.

"Sight Unseen" was written after viewing artist Hank Willis Thomas's 2011 piece *From Cain't See in the Morning Till Cain't See at Night*.

"Elegy for Julius Gaw": The character Julius Gaw appears in the 1989 film *Friday the 13th Part VIII: Jason Takes Manhattan*.

ACKNOWLEDGMENTS

Many thanks to the judges and editors who chose these poems for publication. They appeared for the first time, sometimes in an earlier version, in the following:

Apogee Journal	"When She Asks What I'm Afraid Of"
Auburn Avenue	"Chattanooga Blues"
Hayden's Ferry Review	"Benediction for the Black & Young"
	"When My Days Fill with Ghosts"
Quiddity	"Sight Unseen"
Silver Blade Magazine	"Elegy for Julius Gaw"
TAYO Literary Magazine	"Dear God"
Timber	"DWB"
Voicemail Poems	"How It Feels to Be Black"
Welter	"The Appetite"

The utmost love and gratitude to the following for supporting me and making this work possible:

Curtis and Cheryl Collier, Caitlin Collier, Dr. Cayanna, AJ, Julianna, and Antwan Good, Shane Morrow, James McKissic, Rebecca Palmer, Tyree Daye, Donna Spruijt-Metz, Nick Makouske, Marcus Thomas, Christine Hall, Sybil Baker, J. Ed Marston, Andréana Lefton,

Isaac Duncan, Richard Winham, Ronda Foster, Judith Sachsman, Bao Phi, Wess Mongo Jolley, Ray Bassett, Adera Causey, Henry Lynch, Artsbuild, RISE Chattanooga, the Loft Literary Center, Rhyme-N-Chatt, the University of Tennessee Chattanooga, WUTC, Scenic Trend, The Plug Poetry Project, Ross White, Noah Stetzer, and the entire Bull City staff.

ABOUT THE AUTHOR

Christian J. Collier is a Black, Southern writer, arts organizer, and teaching artist who resides in Chattanooga, Tennessee. His works have appeared or are forthcoming in *Hayden's Ferry Review, Michigan Quarterly Review, Atlanta Review, Grist Journal,* and elsewhere. A 2015 Loft Spoken Word Immersion Fellow, he is also the winner of the 2020 ProForma Contest and the 2019-2020 *Seven Hills Review* Poetry Contest. More about him and his work can be found at *www.christianjcollier.com.*